anythink

D0460787

GUARDING
THE SUPER BOWL STADIUM

BY ELIZABETH WEITZMAN

The
Child's
World®
childsworld.com

Published by The Child's World®
1980 Lookout Drive • Mankato, MN 56003-1705
800-599-READ • www.childsworld.com

Acknowledgments
The Child's World®: Mary Swensen, Publishing Director
Red Line Editorial: Editorial direction and production
The Design Lab: Design

Design Element: Iaroslav Neliubov/Shutterstock Images
Photographs ©: Ross D. Franklin/AP Images, cover, 1, 10; Paul Spinelli/
AP Images, 5; Rich Graessle/Icon Sportswire, 6; Leonard Zhukovsky/
Shutterstock Images, 9; Jed Jacobsohn/AP Images, 12; Andrew Kelly/
Reuters/Corbis, 14; Joe Mahoney/AP Images, 15; Julio Cortez/Corbis, 17;
John Minchillo/AP Images, 19; Alexander Zemlianichenko/AP Images, 20

ISBN 9781503808140
LCCN 2015958278

Printed in the United States of America
Mankato, MN
June, 2016
PA02302

ABOUT THE AUTHOR

Elizabeth Weitzman is a longtime journalist
and the author of more than 25 nonfiction
books for children.

TABLE OF CONTENTS

CHAPTER 1

Super Sunday Safety

Two teams. Sixty minutes of game time. And about a hundred million people watching to see who will take home the trophy. The Super Bowl is the biggest day in football. It determines the season's champion. For many fans, it is the biggest sporting event of the year.

Most fans' eyes are on the field. But there is action everywhere. There is more going on than you realize. Thousands of people work together to pull off a single Super Bowl Sunday.

There are tons of tiny details that have to be just right. The field has to be perfect. The stands have to be clean. A fan might try to sneak onto the field and stop the game. Or the power could suddenly go out.

Some of the most important details involve safety. Safety, or security, is one of the National Football

The Super Bowl draws tens of thousands of fans each year who need to be kept safe.

League's (NFL's) top concerns. Everyone inside
the stadium has to feel safe, from the second the

GATE	SECTION	ROW	SEAT
1	112	17	18

MAIN

SUPER BOWL

XLIX

VINCE LOMBARDI TROPHY

NFL

02.01.15

SUNDAY · FEBRUARY 1, 2015 · 4:00 PM
UNIVERSITY OF PHOENIX STADIUM
ARIZONA

$1750

Stadium Gates Open at Noon
All Taxes Included

SUPER BOWL XLIX
MAIN

GATE	SECTION	ROW	SEAT
1	112	17	18

Visit NFL.com/SBApp to download the Super Bowl GameDay App

963599149192

Fans need a ticket or media credential to get into the big game, but they can be difficult to find and expensive to buy.

doors open until the last piece of confetti has been swept up.

The league goes to great lengths to make sure this happens. Military planes watch over the stadium. There are undercover cops in the stands. Members of the Coast Guard patrol waterways. X-ray machines scan every item that enters.

No one gets in without a **credential** or ticket. These can be hard to get. They can also cost thousands of dollars. Those that get in can consider themselves lucky. But even they do not know everything that is happening. They do not know all of the secret security that keeps everybody safe.

CHAPTER 2

Securing the Stadium

It takes a lot of work to plan a Super Bowl. The first step is choosing a location. This happens about four years in advance. This gives the host city time to prepare to host such a huge event.

Usually, the Super Bowl is held in a warm city. New Orleans and Miami have each hosted ten times. Sometimes the game is held in a cold city. Those stadiums will usually have a roof. The perfect stadium holds at least 70,000 fans. That is a lot of people to keep safe on game day.

Keeping everybody safe is a team effort. This effort starts years in advance. Local police officers start planning security tactics well before the game. Government agencies pitch in and help. The Secret Service, the FBI, federal air marshals, and the Transportation Security Administration

New York police officers on horses patrol Times Square during the week leading up to the Super Bowl after the 2013 season.

(TSA) all work together to protect everyone inside the stadium.

How do they do this? One way is through the air. The Super Bowl after the 2014 season was held at the University of Phoenix Stadium. The New England Patriots played the Seattle Seahawks. It was a classic game. It was close until the end.

Black Hawk helicopters were used to monitor the skies during the Super Bowl after the 2014 season.

Fans' eyes were glued to the field. But there was also a lot happening overhead. F-16 fighter jets and Black Hawk helicopters protected the **no-fly zone** above the stadium. They made sure no aircraft entered the area.

The year before, the Seahawks played the Denver Broncos at MetLife Stadium in New Jersey. That stadium is near canals, creeks, and rivers. That week, Coast Guard boats and dive teams kept those waterways safe. High-tech machines made sure the air was clean. Specially trained dogs sniffed around, searching for bombs. And about 6,000 security guards walked around the stadium itself.

All of this security requires organization. A Super Bowl security command center is set up. It is in a secret location. The center holds police officers, soldiers, and FBI agents. They and other officials watch over the operation. They make sure everything runs smoothly.

The command center is full of great tools. Computers and screens show what is happening in the area. Helicopters fly overhead to provide an aerial view. Giant X-ray machines take pictures of equipment trucks. Undercover detectives in the stands send reports of possible danger. Officers even look on social media Web sites such as

BLOWING THE SECRET

Every Super Bowl requires thousands of hours of planning. But there might be slipups anyway. In 2014, CBS broadcast a show about the great new technology at the Super Bowl command center. It was a secret site with secret technology. So imagine the NFL's surprise when the command center's Wi-Fi password was shown on-screen for millions to see! No doubt it was changed quickly.

The power outage at the Super Bowl after the 2012 season brought with it unique security concerns.

Facebook and Twitter. They look to see if anybody is posting threats.

Each year, the NFL has to deal with new issues. The Super Bowl after the 2012 season had a unique problem. The Baltimore Ravens were playing the San Francisco 49ers. The power went out early in the second half. The stadium was almost completely dark. The game was stopped for more than 30 minutes. Backup generators got the lights back on. Now the NFL monitors host stadiums' power supplies more closely.

CHAPTER 3

Getting Seated

The Super Bowl draws tens of thousands of fans. Many arrive in a host city days before the big game. Some fly and some drive. Others take buses, trains, or subways. Each of these areas needs special attention.

The TSA sends extra officers to local airports. They also send **canine** teams. These are the dogs that sniff around for dangerous materials. They help inspect luggage for items such as bombs.

People driving also face extra security checks. They might have their license plates scanned. This lets officers do a quick

THE GREAT IMPOSTER

Today, guards quickly stop anyone who tries sneaking onto the field. But in the 1980s, Barry Bremen got the best of them. His goal was to go where he did not belong. One of his best attempts was in 1982. That year, he tried to enter the Super Bowl dressed as the San Diego Chicken. Security guards caught him before he got in. But he never lost his nickname: the Great **Imposter.**

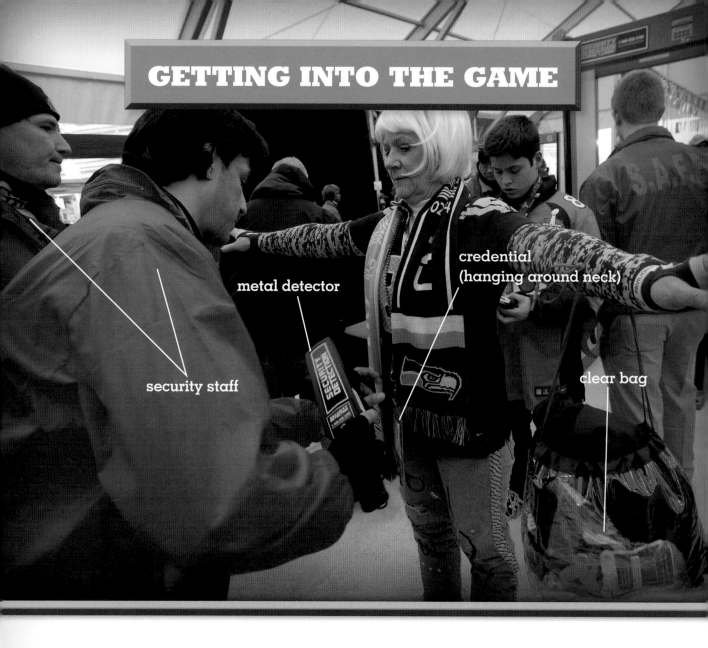

GETTING INTO THE GAME

metal detector

credential (hanging around neck)

security staff

clear bag

background check. Fans taking buses or trains need proof they are going to the game. They have to show their Super Bowl ticket to get to the stadium.

Sometimes this is not so easy. NFL tickets are printed with barcodes. The tickets also have

The NFL introduced a new clear bag policy before the 2013 season.

holograms and special ink. Each one is checked
with a handheld machine. If the machine cannot
read the ticket, the ticket holder is not allowed in.
Many scammers try to sell **counterfeit** tickets.

Some unlucky fans get tricked into buying them. They are turned away at the stadium gates.

Having a real ticket is important. But it is just the start of getting seated.

Going to the Super Bowl can feel like going to the airport. Fans walk through an X-ray machine. Their belongings are scanned by yet another machine. A guard pats down all entrants. It can seem annoying to go through so much trouble. But if it keeps danger away, it is all worth it.

CHAPTER 4

Protecting the Prizes

Fans have to wait in line to get to their seats. The security they have to go through can take a while. But players do not have to worry about that. They have their own bodyguards. The bodyguards will

The Vince Lombardi Trophy is handled carefully before being presented to the winning team.

often ride with the players in a private car from their home or hotel to the stadium. Guards also protect the locker rooms.

There is even security for game-day equipment. All the footballs are taken to the officials' locker room before kickoff. Each one is checked and given an air pressure test. If the balls do not pass, they cannot be used.

While everyone else is focused on the game, a special guard sits inside the stadium waiting for it to end. It is his or her job to protect the Vince Lombardi Trophy. That is what the winning team of the Super Bowl gets. It is presented in a ceremony after the game. The trophy is made by famous jewelers Tiffany & Co. It is kept in a locked box. Anyone who touches the trophy before the ceremony has to wear gloves. That keeps the trophy shiny and free of fingerprints.

The trophy is made from about 7 pounds (3.2 kg) of sterling silver. That makes it quite valuable. But Super Bowl rings are worth more. Each year,

New York Giants owner John Mara shows off the team's ring from the Super Bowl after the 2011 season.

winning teams receive unique rings. Some rings have included more than 200 diamonds.

It takes a team effort to win a Super Bowl. There are a lot of people off the field who help. That is why

New England Patriots owner Robert Kraft (left) accidentally gave his ring from the Super Bowl after the 2004 season to Russian president Vladimir Putin (right).

rings do not just go to the winning players. Team owners, coaches, and front office staff also get them. Sometimes the cheerleaders do, too.

Of course, everyone wants to show off their rings. Some players even wear them after their careers are over. But they are usually hidden in safes or safety deposit boxes. They are worth too much—and are way too heavy—to actually wear around all day.

A Super Bowl trophy and rings can be worth millions of dollars. But there is nothing more valuable than the safety of the fans. The NFL and the different security groups know this. They work hard to make sure Super Bowl Sunday is a fun and safe day for everybody.

KEEPING AN EYE ON THE RINGS

Super Bowl winners need to be careful. Championship rings have a way of disappearing. Green Bay Packer Jerry Kramer left his in an airplane bathroom. Kansas City Chief Frank Pitts had his stolen from his house. Dallas Cowboy Bob Lilly lost his. So did New England Patriot Larry Izzo. But Patriots owner Robert Kraft might have the strangest story. He showed his ring to Russian president Vladimir Putin. Putin kept it! Kraft did not want to create any political problems. So he let Putin have it.

GLOSSARY

background check (BAK-ground CHEK) A background check involves looking up a person's legal history. Police do a quick background check on many people trying to get into the Super Bowl.

canine (KAY-nine) Something is canine if it relates to dogs. The FBI's canine team is trained to find hidden bombs and other explosives.

counterfeit (KOWN-ter-fit) A counterfeit is a fake version of something real. Scammers try to sell counterfeit Super Bowl tickets.

credential (kri-DEN-shul) A credential is an approved pass. You need a ticket or credential to get into the Super Bowl.

federal (FED-er-uhl) Federal groups are groups relating to the national government. Federal air marshals help protect fans during the Super Bowl.

guidelines (GUYD-linez) Guidelines are rules. Make sure you check the guidelines before you bring anything with you to the stadium.

imposter (im-PAW-ster) An impostor is someone who pretends to be someone else. Barry Bremen was nicknamed "the Great Imposter" because he tried to dress up as other people to gain access to the field.

law enforcement (LAW en-FORS-ment) Law enforcement is a group of people whose job it is to protect society from criminals. Super Bowl fans can feel a lot safer knowing police officers and other law enforcement agents are on duty.

no-fly zone (no-FLY ZOHN) A no-fly zone is an area in the sky where planes and other aircraft are not allowed to be without permission. There should not be any unidentified planes in the no-fly zone above the stadium during the Super Bowl.

TO LEARN MORE

IN THE LIBRARY

Encarnacion, Elizabeth. *Sports Stadiums*.
Laguna Hills, CA: QEB Publishing, 2007.

Rogers, Kate. *Air Marshals*. New York: PowerKids Press, 2016.

Streissguth, Thomas. *America's Security Agencies: The Department of Homeland Security, FBI, NSA, and CIA*.
Berkeley Heights, NJ: MyReportLinks.com Books, 2008.

ON THE WEB

Visit our Web site for links about guarding the Super Bowl stadium: **childsworld.com/links**

Note to Parents, Teachers, and Librarians: We routinely verify our Web links to make sure they are safe and active sites. So encourage your readers to check them out!

INDEX